Memories of World War II

Seen through

the eyes of a Dutch teenager

Original title: 'De Jongens van de Diepenveenseweg'

With special thanks to my father, Anne Egbert (Han) van Nijen

Cover by Renate van Nijen
www.renatevannijen.com

Layout Ferry Verhoeve

Table of contents

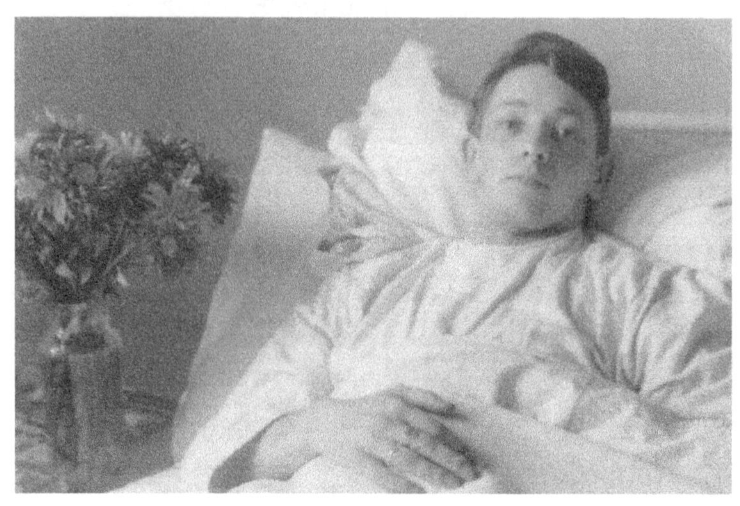

Dedicated to my Uncle Wim, whom I got to know
through the stories in this book

Derk Willem (Wim) van Nijen

04-02-1927   -   25-07-1947

Deventer – The Netherlands

Preface

A house with a story. At the age of eighty-nine, my father, still very fit, came to Spain to celebrate my sixtieth birthday. Whilst we had our breakfast at a seafront cafe, memories started to surface. Memories about his own wartime experiences in the city of Deventer. The past does not let go of every 'secret', but this book gives you an impression of the life of my father and his family during the Second World War in The Netherlands. My father's story is similar to those of many of his generation that will never be heard. I have decided to document these wartime memories in a collection of short stories. For 'Memories of World War II' I mainly describe the events in and near the house where my father's family lived at the time.

I am writing the stories that my dad shared with me in his own words, so in the first person. This way he becomes the narrator of his own memories. In order to write these stories I interviewed my father, Han van Nijen and his brothers Laurens and Fokke. I also received information from Evert Weltevreden, a cousin of my father and the son of 'Uncle Henk', who is mentioned in several chapters in this book. To get a vivid idea about the house, which survived the many bombings on Deventer during the war, I received information from Marion and Joost, the current owners of the house. They sent me videos and photos of the house in which several original features from the past have been preserved. Furthermore, I collected some historical information about the city of Deventer during the war. Through this book I want you to 'experience' some of the events - seen through the eyes of a teenage boy - that turned a normal family in an occupied country during wartime into a family with many unshared secrets.

A piece of history

Deventer, a historical city in the Netherlands, is a so-called 'Hanseatic city'. But what exactly is that? Partly thanks to its strategic location along the banks of the river IJssel, the city was already known as a settlement of merchants during the second half of the 8th century. As one of the oldest cities in the Netherlands, Deventer was trading with Sweden and Norway, but also with England and the German cities of Lübeck, Hamburg and Bremen. In addition to products such as fish, grain and wood, salt and wine were traded. Thanks to its favourable location, Deventer became an important meeting point for overland trade and quickly acquired a market function. Several annual markets were held. This meant that it was important to protect trading activities. It led to Deventer joining the German Hanseatic League, an alliance of merchants who mainly traded in the Baltic Sea. The Hanseatic period was from the thirteenth century to the early fifteenth century. Deventer's strategic location was also one of the main reasons why Nazi Germany wanted to occupy the city.

Diepenveenseweg 1940-1945

My father's family home is located in the Diepenveenseweg in Deventer, at about fifteen hundred metres from the railway bridge that was so important to the German occupiers. The house did incur some damage, such as broken windows and roof tiles, but it was not completely destroyed like so many of the buildings in the city. During the war, Deventer developed an important Resistance movement. My grandfather Fokke van Nijen, my Uncle Wim (officially called Derk Willem), an uncle of my father Henk Weltevreden, Mr. Gerritsma who was the landlord, and my father himself, despite his young age, were also active in the Resistance.

My father was not aware of this at the time. It wasn't until later in life that the pieces of the puzzle fell into place. Many young men and women, such as students from the Colonial Agricultural School, joined the Resistance. My Uncle Wim joined as well. Too many of them lost their lives. Their names are listed on several stone memorials in Deventer, including the name of my Uncle Wim, who died in 1947 from an injury incurred during the Second World War.

Diepenveenseweg May 2019

"It's a warm sunny day in May as my brother Fokke and I drive down the Diepenveenseweg. The Deventer train station is on the left and on the right we see the property, so familiar to us. It was our family home during the war years, 1940-1945. We park the car opposite the house and I notice that it hasn't changed much at all. Only the door has been replaced. There used to be a dark green door with an oval ornamental iron frame in the middle. Now there is a dark grey door with two windows. When we cross the street, we first walk to the gate on the right-hand side. We look at the outside brick wall of the house. The advertising on the wall has been restored to its old glory by the current owners of the building. It says 'Fa. N.J. Gerritsma, Groothandel in Chocolade en Suikerwaren' (chocolate and confectionary wholesale). In between the letters you can still see an even older text 'Groothandel in chocolade, cacao, biscuits, suikerwerken, drops' (chocolate, cocoa, biscuits, confectionery, licorice wholesale').

I remember that there also used to be advertising on the front of the house, just above the windows of the attic. Attached to the roof gutter, there were two billboards with the words 'Tjoklat & Kwatta' (old Dutch chocolate brands) written in large letters.

Marion and Joost, the owners, have invited us to come and have a look at their house. It feels very strange and yet special to be here again after so many years. I feel a mix of curiosity, joy and fear because of the memories which are bubbling up in my head when I look at the large window on the left, which used to be the front room.

Wim is lying in his bed. We were just joking around. He is in a lot of pain because of his back problems, but he is holding up well. Wim is my oldest brother. I am three years younger than him. He is a lot calmer than me as I'm indisputably the rascal in our family. It is difficult for me to understand how he can accept his situation so well. He is very religious. He talks about Jesus as if he is his best friend. It gives him much comfort. He is 18 years old and he was shot in the back. The wound just won't heal. He can barely walk and lies on his bed all day, in the front room on the first floor.

Every day I keep him company for a couple of hours and my endless chatter always makes him laugh.

Today is no different. My youngest brother Fokke is with us, he is four years old and is sitting on the ground playing with some wooden blocks. I walk to the window and look outside. I see the railway platform in front of our house. The station is patrolled by SS soldiers*. Passenger trains are no longer coming in as the transport of people was stopped quite some time ago. Everything has been put to a hold, apart from the occasional German freight train passing by. I look at the billboards and some of the wooden benches and see an SS soldier with a rifle gun in his hands. At some point we look each other straight in the eye. I am feeling mischievous and wave at him. "Weg Dort, weg dort", he shouts angrily, indicating that I have to move away from the window, but I don't listen to him. It all happens in a split second as he points his gun at me and fires. I am totally freaked out. Fortunately, the bullet has missed me and hits the roof gutter. Wim shouts "Get away from that window!"

Wim and I are holding our breath, almost

expecting some German soldiers to knock on our door in order to punish me and to assert their power. We are all very upset. My little brother Fokke is crying. He got really frightened because of the sound of the bullet against the gutter and Wim's shout. We're anxiously waiting to see whether anything else will happen. Minutes pass but it stays calm. I have learned my lesson.

Till this day I can still feel the fear from that moment in the front room. It was very intense. As I look at the window I realise that, as a fourteen-year-old boy, I knew very little about my brother and what had happened to him. Years later, after the war, I heard from my Uncle Henk that my brother Wim had fought for the Resistance and that he eventually died from the injuries sustained during the war.

They never spoke about it at home and I still don't know what role he played in the Resistance, but his name is engraved upon two memorial stones – in Markelo and in Deventer – for Resistance fighters. He can no longer share his secrets, they have ended up buried with him and all those other heroes in silence. Those who witnessed it and were able to retell the story did not want to do so. The past was closed off and hidden in forgotten memories.

- The SS (Schutzstaffel) was founded in 1925 to protect Nazi gatherings, but was later known primarily as a paramilitary organisation commanded by Himmler. They were always dressed in black uniforms and were nicknamed 'De Zwarthemden' (The black shirts) by many people.

The start of the Occupation

My brother Fokke and I walk towards the front door. The property, built in 1896, has been beautifully renovated and maintained by the current owners. The soft yellow window frames form a nice contrast against the brick walls. I look at the subtle stained-glass windows above the two large windows on the ground floor and above the front door. They display a beautiful white flower design. Above it there is a narrow, ornate piece of ironwork, framed by the red and orange bricks. I am sure they have always been there, but as a young man, I was not aware of that sort of detail. I do remember that there was a letterbox slot built into the brick wall next to the door. I cannot see it now, but perhaps this is because of the lush plant with white flowers placed in front of it.

There is a tree in front of the house, which was not there when I lived here. Neither were there any plants beneath the windows. I remember that there was ivy climbing gracefully up the right side of the house. Our family lived on the first floor. Mr. Gerritsma, our landlord, lived on the ground floor. We could push up the sash wooden window frames in our living and dining room. I can still see myself hanging out of the window on a beautiful sunny day, watching the trains that passed by, or stopped to allow passengers to get in and out. There used to be green wooden shutters next to the windows, which we always closed at night. I also remember the dormer very well, as it was in the attic, where I slept with my brothers Henk and Laurens.

We walk up the two steps to the front door and are warmly welcomed by Marion and Joost. My brother Fokke and I immediately notice that the tiles of the floor in the hall are still the original ones. Mosaic tiles, so typical of the style of that time, with dark red, white, pale yellow and blue squares and triangles, also called Spanish or Portuguese tiles. The tiled floor turns to the right just before the stairs, but we enter the living room to the right of the hallway. I get a flashback and my mind wanders off.

I'm standing outside behind the fence that gives access to the garage on the side of the house, with my brothers Wim and Henk. The fence is still there, but it used to be an iron fence with bars, now it is a wooden gate. My mother is standing in the hallway and my father and Mr. Gerritsma are standing in Mr. Gerritsma's office, which is now the living room. I am ten years old. The front door is open. We watch and listen to the footsteps of a regiment of German soldiers. The leather army boots form a rhythmic basis to which the Germans are singing. "Wir fahren nach England" (We are going to England). I'm looking at the rifles on their backs.

We are just standing there in disbelief and defeat. They are on their way to Olst, but it doesn't take long for that same regiment of Germans to come back and pass our house once again, as apparently they cannot walk any further. It is very surreal.

My second youngest brother Laurens is still asleep because our mother hadn't woken him up that morning. When he eventually awakens, it is to the strange, loud rhythmic sound of the marching boots. He comes down the stairs into the hallway, where he sees a lot of suitcases and bags. Mother had prepared him a sandwich that she gives to him.

Laurens remembers this moment well, as he told me recently, because he was very impressed with all those bags and suitcases in the hallway, not to mention the pushchair in the middle, with our youngest brother Fokke in it. Our parents had prepared everything in case we had to leave the house in a rush. Fortunately, it did not come to that. In the end, it wasn't necessary to evacuate. I can still recall the mixture of fear and excitement that I felt at the time. Laurens says he was lying on the floor in the office, where he could see the Germans' boots through the air vents. That entire afternoon it was a coming and going of entire regiments of German soldiers. It was impressive and very frightening at the same time. The German invasion was a reality.

On the tenth of May, Germany invaded the east of the Netherlands. This invasion did not come as a surprise to Deventer nor to the rest of the Netherlands. As early as 1936, Dutch police forces were working together with the military police. Defence lines were put into place and the 'IJssel linie', which was meant to resist the imminent invasion, was set up. Bridges were equipped with explosives and Steenenkamer and De Worp, districts of Deventer, were evacuated in order to create minefields.

On the other side of the river IJssel 'casemates' were built. These are concrete bunkers. The Deventer defences looked strong. The city was ready to withstand attack. At first it seemed as if the Germans could be stopped by blowing up two of the three arches of the railway bridge on May 10, 1940. This was accomplished by the Dutch, but they were taken by surprise when the Germans used an armoured train to punch a hole in their defence. Without slowing down, they simply crashed the Deventer defence line and managed to cross the river at the city of Zutphen. A day later the battle was over and the occupation of Deventer and its immediate surroundings became a reality.

The surprising Mr. Gerritsma

We are treated to a cup of coffee in the living room. The windows at the front look exactly like they did during the war and the French doors to the courtyard are still the same as back then. I remember this space very well, it was Mr. Gerritsma's office. He had a wholesale business in confectionery and was our landlord.

Nicolaas Johannes Gerritsma was born in Friesland, a province in the north of the Netherlands, but when he was thirty-five years old he moved to Deventer. He was a slender, tall, striking-looking man, who always walked with a straight back. I can still see his narrow, elongated face and his thick white hair in my mind's eye. He had very dark eyebrows and wore silver-framed half-moon glasses. I got on really well with him and I liked him, because he was always cheerful.

Even before we moved to the house in the Diepenveenseweg, my brothers and I often visited him and his then wife. We always got some treats and were allowed to play in the large garden, which was a great adventure for us. At that time we lived in the Goldenbeltstraatje, a street close to the Diepenveenseweg. We moved to the Goldenbeltstraatje when we had to leave De Worp in 1937. I'm not sure, but I suspect this was because all the inhabitants of De Worp were evacuated around that time, due to the impending war.

My Uncle Henk Weltevreden and his wife, Aunt Annie, who was one of my mother's sisters, also lived in the Goldenbeltstraatje in a building owned by Mr. Gerritsma. Ome Henk worked as a representative at the confectionary wholesaler and he drove all over the country in a T-Ford van. In 1938, Mr. Gerritsma's wife died and he decided not to live on his own in the large building. He had children, but they had already left the house, so he asked my parents if they wanted to move in with him and live on the first floor and the attic.

Every day he came to our dining room to enjoy lunch with us. At the time, this was the main meal of the day, usually consisting of meat, potatoes, vegetables and gravy. There was a large kitchen on the ground floor and you could get there by turning right in the hallway, just before the staircase leading to the first floor. Before reaching the kitchen you had to walk past a door to the basement, which played such an important role towards the end of the war.

My mother was a very good cook and could prepare a delicious meal from very few ingredients and Mr. Gerritsma really enjoyed having lunch with us. In the evening, he would make a sandwich for himself downstairs. There were sliding doors in the office that gave access to the main bedroom where he slept. He had built a small kitchen block in his bedroom where he could make coffee and prepare his breakfast and evening meal. The sliding doors are no longer there; the bedroom is now a modern kitchen.

The French doors to the courtyard behind the gate bring back memories. This courtyard gave access to a spacious garage, where the T-Ford van, an old 1930 Dodge, that Gerritsma used to drive, and a number of bicycles were kept. Next to the garage was a small staircase of just two steps with a sliding door to a very large warehouse leading all the way to the back of the house, where a large door gave access to the Goldenbeltstraatje. This door is still there.

The warehouse was used for the

confectionery business. The goods were loaded and unloaded through the door in the Goldenbeltstraatje. There was an equally large space above the warehouse and it was filled to the brim with furniture. One day, I was snooping around the house, I saw this furniture. Antique wardrobes, tables, chairs, clocks... I could not believe my eyes. "Mum, why is there so much furniture in the space above the warehouse?" I asked my mum. "Sssh" she said, "you can never tell anybody, never, you hear me? Just forget about it, pretend you haven't seen it, but absolutely never, ever talk to anyone about it. Not with your friends, not with your brothers, not at school, not even with the teacher at school, with nobody at all, understood?"

Years later, after the war, I heard from my Uncle Henk that this was furniture owned by Jewish people who were either in hiding or had already been taken to concentration camps. Their friends had stored their furniture above the warehouse. After the war, the furniture was returned to their rightful owners, if they had survived the war, or to surviving relatives.

In the early years of the war, from 1940 to 1943 and also for a part of 1944, life continued as normal. We, my brothers and I, went to school every day and the confectionery wholesale continued doing business. We were aware of the war, because although it was relatively quiet, there was the daily rumble of heavy bombers of the Allies flying over Deventer in the direction of Germany. This had already started in the beginning of the war. These bomber planes were always accompanied by 'Spitfires', small fighter planes of the English, which had to protect the big bombers, so we were told. I think that as many as 40 bombers a day flew over, but you got used to the sound.

Only towards the end of the war, at the beginning of 1945, we were no longer allowed to go to school, because it had become too dangerous. However, I did get organ lessons from my Uncle Henk. He was an organist in a local church. I often played on the organ we had at home. My father liked to play on it as well, but he could only play two hymns. Funny how something like that stays with you.

During those early years of the war, I was sometimes allowed to join Mr. Gerritsma in the beautiful Dodge to go to a cake factory in Terborg. I loved that. Mr. Gerritsma sang songs, passionately and loudly, as we drove through the landscape at forty kilometres per hour. There weren't many cars on the road and everybody was looking at us. At the factory, he went to the manager to buy cake for the wholesale business.

I was then allowed to take home some so-called 'kantkoek'. The cakes in the factory were cut into perfectly square pieces and the edges that fell off were called 'kantkoek'. They were collected in large barrels. This was normally thrown away, but the guys at the factory would say to me, "Take what you want, boy." So, I filled a really big bag with as many pieces of cake as I could squeeze in. It was always a real treat. On my way back to Deventer in the Dodge I usually ate so much of it that I was nauseous and had diarrhoea for three days. But there was also a lot left for the rest of the family. I cherish this memory, except for the diarrhoea of course!

In 1944, the Dodge and the T-Ford van were seized by the Germans. The Dodge had already been taken apart and all the valuable parts removed by my Uncle Henk. The Germans took it anyway, because they could use anything.

The last year of the war, Mr. Gerritsma went to sleep in his office and my brothers Henk, Laurens and I, were allowed to sleep in his bedroom on the ground floor as it had become too dangerous to stay in the attic where we used to sleep. At this time my brother Wim was already injured and could hardly walk anymore, he was lying in the living room on the first floor. There were also two bedrooms and a dining room on the first floor. My parents slept in one of those bedrooms with my youngest brother Fokke and the other bedroom was rented out to a lady called Gre. Unfortunately, I don't remember her last name. She was the director at a local supermarket, called the EPA. Gre always had her meals with us.

The reason why we were allowed to sleep in Gerritsma's bedroom was because this way we could quickly run to the basement to hide for the bombings during an air raid alarm, which happened with great regularity during the second half of 1944. I always helped my father to carry my brother Wim down to the basement on a kitchen chair, because he couldn't walk down the stairs himself. Gerritsma never went into the basement. I believe because he didn't mind dying, but I am not totally sure about that.

At the beginning of 1944 we were evacuated for a number of months. At the time Wim was already working for the Resistance and he stayed at the home of a milkman, with whom he also worked. This was before he got injured. The rest of us stayed with an elderly couple in the Tuinstraat, five hundred metres behind our house. I don't remember whether Mr. Gerritsma was there as well. All the houses in our street were evacuated. This was ordered by the Germans because they wanted us to leave the station area. I suspect this was because freight wagons with ammunition regularly entered the station and they often stopped in front of our house for hours on end. These trains became a target for the Allies, so it was too dangerous to stay in our house. By this time all the Jews had already been transported.

During this evacuation I still went home every day to feed Trixie, our little dog who stayed in the garage. Because she was so lonely, we also got a cat to keep Trixie company. Sadly the little cat only lived for three months. She became so sick that we had to put her to sleep at the vet. Trixie didn't really get the best kind of food during that period and her legs grew all crooked, but she survived the war and eventually died when she was ten years old. After the evacuation, we were allowed to return home.

The last winter of the war, in January and February 1945, we slept in the basement. Gre also slept in the basement with us. The rest of the house had become too dangerous, as there were many bombardments by the Allies who targeted the railway bridge. My parents had made a bed for Wim in the back of the basement. Mr. Gerritsma never slept in the basement. I got the impression that he didn't know fear.

Mr. Gerritsma loved to speak Frisian, his mother tongue. My Uncle Henk learned the Frisian language from him so that they could converse together in Frisian. He often made an old Frisian main course called 'Potstro'. Many called it 'Luie Wievenkost' (food for lazy wives) because it was so easy to make. Boy, that was so good. Just thinking about it makes my mouth water.

We never got hungry during the war. We ate that 'potstro' once a week and everyone really liked it. It was made from buckwheat flour with buttermilk and then a hollow was made in it, to which bacon and bacon fat were added.

Mr. Gerritsma survived the war and we rebuilt our lives. All the damage to the house was repaired. After the large windows were damaged for the first time due to heavy bombings, they were replaced by wooden panels with a small window in it, by my Uncle Henk. After the war they were restored to their old glory with the stained-glass parts above them. Our family went back upstairs and Mr. Gerritsma was able to sleep in his own bedroom on the ground floor again.

I have a lot of warm memories of this special

man whom I considered to be a good friend. The first December after the war, I was fifteen, we celebrated Sinterklaas* together. Mr. Gerritsma was Sinterklaas and I was his helper, 'zwarte Piet'. My entire face was blackened and I put on the colourful 'zwarte piet' outfit. We went to the EPA store to give presents and treats to little children and we also went to surprise and give some gifts and treats to my youngest brother Fokke, who was five years old at the time. Later that day Fokke told my mother "Zwarte Piet was wearing Han's shoes, Mamma!"

Gerritsma did not retire until the age of eighty-eight. He had run his wholesale business for sixty years. He lived until the fine old age of ninety-three and died on January 26, 1976.

*Sinterklaas (also called 'Sint Nicolaas') is not the same as Santa Claus and has nothing to do with Christmas. Every year he is celebrated on the 5th of December in the Netherlands and on the 6th in Belgium. His helper is called 'zwarte Piet' (black Peter). Sinterklaas arrives in the Netherlands at the end of November on a boat coming from Spain. He has a white horse that can walk across the roof tops. Small children can leave one of their shoes in front of the chimney before going to bed and the next day there will be a present from Sinterklaas in their shoe.

Wartime food

The kitchen on the ground floor was very spacious. On the left there was a large iron stove that my mother used to cook on in the winter. During the summer months she cooked on a gas ring attached to butane gas bottles. The kitchen sink was to the right of the iron stove. Past the sink there were white wooden-framed, glass French doors, leading to a small courtyard around four metres square. Immediately outside the door was a roof one metre wide so you stayed dry when it rained and you had to walk to the garage. On the right in the small courtyard there was a coal-shed with coal for the stove and on the left was the lavatory, an outdoor toilet. The toilet's water pipe always froze during the winter months, so as soon as this happened the water was closed off. You then, if you had to go to the bathroom, had to take a bucket of water and salt from the kitchen to wash away your waste. Everyone in the house had to use this one toilet.

In the the middle of the kitchen was the large table, where we sometimes ate together, but most of the time we ate in the dining room on the first floor. On the first floor there was also a large bathroom with a bathtub and a sink. There was no toilet. However, there was a table with a four-pit gas stove that worked on gas. This is where my mother used to cook most of the time. The bathtub was not used. Shelves were laid on the bath and there my mother had stored the plates, spoons, forks, knives and other utensils and spices she used to prepare our meals.

The first few years of the war it was relatively easy to buy food. Next to the warehouse door in the Goldenbeltstraatje were two houses that were also owned by Mr. Gerritsma. My Uncle Henk and Aunt Annie lived in one of those two houses and we used to live in the other house before the war. On the other side of Gerritsma's warehouse was a corner house with a grocery store where you could still buy everything during the first years of the war. Nothing was packaged and the peas, fresh vegetables, chocolate, sugar, and all sorts of other groceries were all stored in crates and boxes, like a market stall. But as of 1944, food became scarce.

My father was working as a collector for the Dutch Association for the Blind and regularly went to the countryside to collect. He always came back with a lot of food, such as eggs, beans and bacon. In particular, the bacon was used once a week by Mr. Gerritsma to make 'Potstro' for the entire family. He really had become part of our family.

I also remember that I went out to nearby farmers to steal tubers with friends. We would take home about 10 tubers each. Although food had become scarce in those last few years, I can't remember ever going hungry. Stealing tubers was more about doing something exciting. I don't think I have ever been punished for this by my parents. It was a time of survival and everything we could eat was used.

Every now and then I went to the so-called 'soup kitchen' with my father and my brother Laurens, I think we mainly got soup and stew there. This must have been during those weeks when my parents had not been able to get food from a farm. A soup kitchen was a place where you could get a hot meal free or for very little money during the war. These were often set up as the initiative of charitable organisations or churches, in many ways like today's food banks.

In the courtyard from the kitchen there was also a door to the garage and in the garage there was a door to the large garden behind the house. In the back of the garden there was a small gazebo where my parents often sat during the summer months. It was a wonderful garden for us to play in. There was also a high hedge with a passage created by my father and uncle that gave access to the garden of my Uncle Henk and unt Annie.

Despite the war, we had a fairly carefree childhood in those early years. We even had a dog called Girlfriend. She was a yellow Dutch shepherd dog who we had found wandering the streets. We really loved that animal. She had a litter once and luckily we found a good home for all the puppies. Girlfriend died in 1944, but I don't remember how. Someone then gave us Trixie, the little dog who lived in the garage during the last year of the war.

All I have is nice memories of the garden. When you walked into the garden there was a morello cherry tree on the left. The cherries were used by my mother to make jam. There were also two lilac trees, a white and a blue one. In the middle of the garden there was a very large pear tree. It was my job to pick the pears. I always climbed into the tree to pick them. The tree gave many buckets full of pears every year, so pear jam and cooked pears were on the menu all year round. Furthermore, close to the pear tree there were four red currant bushes and two gooseberry bushes. Again, my mother made jam out of all of them, but when the berries were ripe we also ate them fresh with home-made curd, made from fresh milk, straight from the cow.

I even remember how my mother made it. She first made buttermilk by churning soured cream. The butter was scooped off and what remained was an acidic liquid, the buttermilk. This was then poured into a bucket through a tea towel. The milk slowly seeped through the towel and what was left in the tea towel was the curd, it tasted like yogurt. This must have been during the first years of the war, because I don't think there was any fresh milk in 1944.

My father had also put two large poles in the ground near the pear tree, with a big stick in between the poles. The rugs from the house were hung over the structure to beat them with a carpet beater. Great to get rid of your frustration.

A lot of memories are surfacing when I think of the garden. During the war, my father grew tobacco in the garden, beneath a couple of old pieces of glass. When the leaves reached the right size, they were picked and dried on top of the stove. My dad used to smoke cigarettes from the tobacco, rolled in brown tissue paper. That's how I learned to smoke. Secretly, because of course I was not allowed to. I was about fourteen years old, I stole some leaves and a cigarette paper and made a cigarette. I didn't like it at all, but I did feel very grown-up. I have no idea whether my parents knew about it, they never said anything, but I must have smelled of tobacco even though I used to smoke outside, never inside, and always alone.

It wasn't until the war had started that we began to breed rabbits. There were three big pens for them in the garage and I was instructed by my parents to take care of them. We had decided to keep the rabbits in the garage and not in the garden, because people in wartime can become desperate and resort to crime. For example, my Uncle Henk and Aunt Annie had a very big rabbit in a pen in their garden which they wanted to keep until Christmas, but just before Christmas the rabbit was stolen.

I was only thirteen years old when my uncle taught me how to slaughter rabbits. We had two bucks and five does. They were Flemish Giant rabbits. I put them together very often and especially towards the end of the war we ate rabbit almost every day. I had to slaughter a rabbit at least once a week, sometimes more often, because there wasn't much else to eat. I can still hear my mother, "Han, can you please slaughter a rabbit?" It had become something very normal to me to just walk into the garage and slaughter a rabbit. Right now it feels strange and I don't know whether I still could do it, but back then it was very common and frankly a necessity. Our neighbours and also my mother and my Aunt Annie saved potato peels and these were given to the rabbits. We also gave them fresh grass and dandelions if they were available and sometimes carrots, but they were too scarce at the end of the war and usually eaten by ourselves.

My mother also regularly went to farmers in the village of Wilp, via De Worp, on foot, to buy things to eat, because food in the city had become quite scarce. She took the old-fashioned perambulator with my youngest brother Fokke, but my brother Laurens and I also came with her. We had to cross the river IJssel, which was strictly controlled by the Germans. Everyone always had to show everything they were carrying and it was forbidden to go and get food from farmers on the other side of the river. However, with my little brother in the pram and with her young boys on either side of her, my mother was always allowed to cross the bridge. The pram was an old model and had lots of space in the bottom, which did not really show from the outside. It was a five or six-mile walk from Deventer to Wilp. Even though it was forbidden, my mother smuggled potatoes, apples, carrots and other vegetables, if they were available, as well as rye flour. All were hidden in the lower part of the pram. We had to walk across the pontoon bridge. This is, simply put, a bridge consisting of a large number of flat barges that lie against each other in the length of the river, with a road surface on it. On the shore sides, the so-called 'headlands', the road surface was fixed to the mainland.

At high tide, which happened regularly, it was a particularly steep walk up to get onto the pontoon bridge and a steep walk down again to reach the other side of the river. Loaded with potatoes and vegetables, the pram was very heavy and we had to help push it, as unobtrusively as possible, to avoid raising suspicion. For me these trips to the farmers were always an exciting adventure. I don't remember whether I was aware that it was also pretty dangerous. The farmers where we got the food were very kind to my brothers and myself and we always got something extra, such as a piece of fruit, when it was in season.

I now realise that, as a family in Deventer, we were very lucky to always have something to eat. During the Dutch 'Winter of Hunger', from September 1944 to April 1945, until the Liberation, people often walked from Amsterdam to the province of Twente in the east of the Netherlands to get fruit and vegetables. They then slept at a farm before walking back. A relative of my father, who grew up on a farm, remembers a young mother with three small children who had walked to the village of Wilp from Amsterdam to get food. This is more than 70 miles. It is almost impossible to imagine, although similar situations are still a reality for many adults and children around in many poorer parts of the world today.

A family in the Resistance

I hear voices down the hall and walk down stairs, I'm curious. I see Willem Jan and Jaap Tensen, known to everyone as the Brothers Tensen. They regularly come to our house and I am always very impressed by them. "Hey Han, how are you doing, pal?" says Jaap with a friendly smile and Willem Jan gives me a pat on the back. They're big and strong and have friendly faces. Willem Jan has a cleft lip, but he doesn't seem to be bothered by that. They are always very kind to me and make me feel part of their group. That makes me feel good. My father, Mr. Gerritsma, my brother Wim and the Brothers Tensen go into the kitchen. They look serious. "Han, go upstairs, go help your mum," says dad, and I do what he says.

I believe this was the moment when, as a thirteen-year-old boy, I realised that my father, my brother Wim and Mr. Gerritsma were doing something that was forbidden. I felt rather proud. I had heard of the Resistance and as young boys all my friends and I at school really disliked the Germans, but there was never really any specific talk about the war. Certainly not at our house and I knew, as a teenage boy, that I could not ask questions about it, so I never did. Not even after the war. I do regret that now. People did not want to talk about it anymore.

When the war was over, I heard that both the brothers were executed. Willem Jan was only twenty-five years old and Jaap twenty-four. They could not stand injustice and always had a kind word for everyone, and this was certainly also my experience. It was only recently, during the creation of this book, that I found out more about their fate and it has reinforced my memory of these brave men. They were from Haerst, a hamlet that is part of the town of Zwolle in the province of Overijssel. I also found a photo on the internet of Jan Willem with Piet Stil, who was a teacher from Rotterdam. During the Second World War Piet often visited, and was even a permanent resident for a while, on 'De Schip'. This was a barge hidden in the reeds, near the mouth of the river Vecht, which was used by a group of Resistance fighters from Zwolle. Allies from shot-down planes were temporarily housed in the barge until they found a safe way to return them to England. There were also other people who were in hiding and the Brothers Tensen often paid the barge a visit. A lot of people knew about the barge and it is indeed very special that those on the barge were never betrayed. Piet was arrested at one point, but he managed to escape and then went into hiding.

Apparently Jaap Tensen said "The Germans will never get us", but quite shortly after that things went wrong. There was a Jewish man hiding in the Tensen family home. When the Germans arrived for a raid in Haerst, the brothers were both at home and decided to flee through the back door into a pasture next door, in the hope that they would not be seen immediately.

The Jewish man, Hans Marius Koopal from Amsterdam, who was twenty-four years old, was hiding somewhere in a hole beneath the hedge, but instead of staying put, he started to run as well, probably in a panic, towards Willem Jan and Jaap. He couldn't run as fast as the brothers and was quickly caught and almost beaten to death on the spot. Two groups of German soldiers shot at Jan Willem and Jaap, they had to lie down in the field to avoid shots, but the Germans caught up with them and they were arrested.

Hans Marius was shot dead on October 3, 1944, along with five other people. Jaap and Willem Jan were executed on October 13, 1944, alongside five other citizens. It is very difficult for me to talk about this because I remember them so well.

Although it was never discussed at my home, I knew my family was part of the Resistance, especially towards the end of the war. For example, my father and my Uncle Henk used to listen to 'Radio Oranje', a Dutch radio programme that was broadcast to the Netherlands from London, via BBC World Service during the war. They were short broadcasts with current affairs and news, including snippets about the Dutch Armed Forces who were fighting the Germans. The first 'Radio Oranje' broadcast was on July 28, 1940. It was a speech by Queen Wilhelmina and it was strictly forbidden by the Germans to listen to this.

All the radios had to be handed in, but my parents didn't comply. They had an old radio which they stored in Uncle Henk's house. My uncle had removed all the wiring and the radio amplifier was placed on the organ in their living room. When people came to visit they often asked how come my uncle had a radio. During the war you never knew who was 'wrong' and who was collaborating with the Germans, and so my uncle used to say "Oh, that's an old antique radio, it doesn't work anymore, but it has sentimental value to us. Look, there's not even wiring attached to it."

It was an antique radio from 1935 and the large square speaker that belonged to it was hidden somewhere in our house. When there was a broadcast by 'Radio Oranje', my father walked through the garden with the loudspeaker to my uncle's house and there they connected the wiring again to listen to the broadcast.

I remember being allowed to come along one day. This was probably towards the end of the war and I was very impressed with the words of our Queen, being broadcast into the room through the loudspeaker. "You know how much faith I put into the resiliance of our entire population. Keep collaborating as a united spirit. Support each other and continue to help everyone else..." I felt very important and grown up, even though I could not have been older than fourteen.

Life went on during the war and even in 1944 I continued to go to school and be mischievous. I clearly remember, that on my way to school with a friend, we had to pass a viaduct and very often there stood an NSB member, selling the NSB newspaper called 'Volk en Vaderland' (People and Motherland). NSB stood for National Socialist Movement. It was a political party from 1931 to 1945 that collaborated with the Germans during World War II. The NSB member was an old man and my friend and I were fast runners so we knew he could never get hold of us. Every time we saw him standing there, on our way to school, we loudly sang "On the corner of the street there is a Pharisee, he is not a human being, he is not an animal, but an NSB, with his newspaper in his hand he is standing there peddling, his 'People and

Motherland, for a few rotten pennies'. He always got furious and tried to run after us, but we were careful and made sure that he couldn't catch us.

Something else that is still, to this day, etched into my memory, are the Jews in the cattle wagons who often stood still for a while, right in front of our house. My younger brother Laurens and I would be given some food from our mother, to share with them. I know this happened a few times. Our parents could not do this themselves as adults, but they trusted that the Germans would not harm young children as they normally didn't. My father would say to us, "Go give some bread to those people in the wagons, boys." We would climb over the fence and walk towards the bars in the wagon. Every thirty metres there was a German soldier to guard the trains, so that the Jews would not escape. Usually these were older men, not SS soldiers, because they were much stricter and would surely have sent us back home. The Jewish people looked at us and put their hands through the bars, I think this must have been in 1943. We would more or less throw the bread at them. We were very close but could not completely reach them. They looked grateful, but they didn't say a word.

These are memories that I would rather forget, because even as a teenage boy I knew that this was inhumane and degrading. The German soldiers just let us do our thing. I already had the feeling that some Germans didn't want to be there at all and I can now imagine that they had no choice. Later I did read stories about German soldiers who refused to shoot people and were then shot themselves.

What I also remember very well is that the Germans had set a curfew during the occupation, from eight o'clock in the evening to four o'clock in the morning. These were hours when the population, especially at night, was not allowed to go outside. The curfew hours were changed and adapted very often. People who had to work at night needed a special permit from the Germans, this was called a 'Sonderausweis' and I very strongly suspect that my father had managed to obtain such an 'Ausweis', as it was also called. He often went out during the curfew. He had also managed not to have to hand in his bicycle, which was quite an achievement.

My father went out, both during the day and in the evening, to collect for the Association for the Blind. The Germans regularly carried out raids. Simply put, these were organized manhunts, organized in peacetime by the government and during wartime by the Occupying forces, to track down and pick up groups of people. My father was stopped very often, but he was always allowed to pass and to continue walking or cycling. Somehow, my father managed to get away with everything he did.

I don't know how he did it, but my father was a smooth talker and with great charm he was able to convince people to get things done. He also went everywhere by train and often took his bicycle on the train. My dad used his bicycle to go and get rye flour from farms that were in the close vicinity of Deventer as well. I can still remember his bicycle. It was an Empo bike with pneumatic tyres and no one else was allowed to ride it. The bicycle had flat tyres very often and I had to repair them again and again, because I had been instructed by my parents to maintain both my father's bicycle as well as the other bicycles that stood in the garage.

There was a bicycle with wooden tyres in the garage as well. Those tyres did bounce a little and the wooden outer tyre had an iron protection, very similar to those on cartwheels. I think this was also called a 'ploffiets' (plop bicycle). If you were driving along a road with boulders or pavers, and there were many at the time, it was like your entire body was being rebuilt. You were completely shaken up. Furthermore, there was a bicycle with garden hoses in the rims. The hoses did not have air in them. This was my Uncle Henk's bicycle and I think there was also a bicycle belonging to my mother. I don't recall whether she used it during the war. I do know that they were all old bicycles that needed a lot of repairs.

I was also allowed to use a bicycle, one with pneumatic tyres. It was smaller than my father's bicycle. Because there was less and less material available during the war, people became very inventive. Rubber was an imported product and therefore scarce. Most of it had already been taken by the Germans. Some people, so I've heard, even used a child's scooter wheel as a front wheel, which was handy, because those kind of weird-looking bicycles were not seized by the Germans.

You needed a special permit to ride a bicycle, so my father must have had such a permit for his work as a collector for the Blind Association, but Resistance fighters also forged those permits, so who knows, he might have had a false permit. We will never know.

I myself, unknowingly, also became a pawn in the Resistance. With a certain regularity, a few times a month, I was told to go to the nearby village of Schalkhaar on my bicycle. This was always when it was dark and sometimes even during the curfew. Schalkhaar was located about three kilometres from Deventer. I had to take a bag of rye flour to a bakery in Schalkhaar and I then received a rye bread from the baker in return. I wasn't told anything, just that I had to go to the bakery with a bag of rye flour in order to get a loaf of bread. I knew very well that there was something important in the bag, but not exactly what. I think I was thirteen or fourteen years old.

Later I understood that my parents sent me because I was still a child and because children were treated less harshly by the Germans and were usually allowed to move on. I don't actually remember ever being stopped. I rarely met anyone during my trips to the bakery, because most people stayed inside. But, one night, there was no moon and no light at all. It was really completely dark and I crashed into another cyclist. We both fell to the ground, but we immediately got back on our bicycles and quickly pedalled away without saying anything. When I arrived at the bakery, I told the baker what had happened to me. He didn't ask whether I was okay, but said very worriedly "And the rye flour, Han, do you still have the rye flour?" I could hear the fear in his voice and that was the moment I realised I was doing something secret, something that might have been forbidden. "Yes I have, here's the bag of rye flour" I said. The baker was clearly relieved.

Years later, I heard from my Uncle Henk that there were messages from the Resistance in the bags, perhaps forged documents from or for people in hiding.

At one point there was also a young man hiding in our house for a number of months. This was when we were back in our house, after the evacuation in the beginning of 1944. He wasn't a Jewish man, he was a Resistance fighter. He had a brother, who also worked for the Resistance, but who got shot and the Germans were looking for him. He had to go into hiding. I remember him very clearly, but unfortunately, I forget his name.

He always ate with us, so he could lead a fairly normal life. At that time we always had our meals at the big table in the kitchen downstairs. He would sleep in my parent's bedroom and my parents went to sleep in the dining room with my brother Fokke. During that same period, Mr. Gerritsma and my parents were obliged by the Germans to give a room in the house to the secretary of the Ortskommandant (local commander). As a family, you had no choice. If you were ordered by the Germans to house someone, this simply had to happen and we were living in a large house.

This secretary slept in the former living room. She used to go home at weekends. Gre was also still renting a room at the time and she was sleeping in the middle room. My brothers and I were sleeping downstairs in Mr. Gerritsma's bedroom and he slept in his former office. The secretary never had her meals with us. I also forget her name. I think she was somewhere between twenty-two and twenty-five years old. She lived with us for a few months, at around the same time as the Resistance fighter.

The stairs that run up from the first floor to the attic had a few creaking steps, I remember that well. As we walk up the stairs, now, to see the rest of the house with Marion, I notice they don't make any sound anymore. Memories are flooding back, because when the secretary was washing herself in the bathroom - we washed ourselves with water in a washtub at the time - I tried to go to the attic unnoticed, so I had to bypass those creaking steps. In the attic, right next to the handrail of the stairs, there was a small hole. Through that hole, which came out in a corner of the bathroom, I could see exactly what was happening in the bathroom. I did this regularly. Of course, I had to be very quiet and careful so she wouldn't hear me. If I suspected she might notice something, I'd quickly slip up the roof and sat there behind the chimney. I can still hear my mother shouting ... "Han, what are you doing there in the attic?"

One day I came out of school and walked past the secretary's room. The door was slightly open and I peeked through the opening. I saw that the secretary was lying in bed with the Resistance fighter. They were obviously in love. During the war, ordinary citizens were also obliged to work for the Germans. So I doubt this lady was part of the NSB. If she had been, she would have betrayed our Resistance fighter, and with him my entire family. Maybe she was in the Resistance and played an important double role.

We can only guess at it because the truth

can no longer be traced. However, I do remember that I was quite surprised when I saw them lying in bed together and I walked to the kitchen where my parents were. I told them what I had seen and my parents just said "Ssssssh, don't say anything Han, never tell anyone". The Resistance fighter was only with us for three months or so and I suspect he was then taken to another hiding address. The secretary also did not stay with us for very long. After she left I never saw her again.

The feeling I get, now that all these memories are surfacing, is that there were also many good people in the Netherlands, who risked their own lives to help others. So did my own family.

Wim

"See you tomorrow," I am waving goodbye to Martin Groeneveld, my best friend. We just walked back from school to our homes together. I throw my school bag on the floor in the hallway and want to close the door behind me, but from the corner of my eyes I see that Wim is arriving back home from school as well. Wim is not alone, but with two boys from the Public School. Martin and I are studying at a Christian High School and Wim at a Technical School, where he is training to be an electrician. When they are in front of our door, I see that Wim is being pushed and they are shouting swear words at him. I feel an incredible anger bubbling up and I run back onto the street. Wim quickly slips past me into the house and with clenched fists, I hit the two guys wherever I can hit them. They soon run off with their tails between their legs. I shout at them "Don't you ever touch my brother again, otherwise you will have to deal with me!" It takes me a while to let go of my anger and calm down. The next day, on my way to school, I see one of those guys walking in the street. He has a thick black eye. "That'll teach him," I think to myself.

My brother Wim and I really got on well. He was called Wim in the family, but his official name was Derk Willem. I was three years younger than him, but we were buddies, despite the fact that he was very different from me. I remember going to gymnastics every week, just before the war, and I was regularly involved in fights. Wim, on the other hand, was very quiet and gentle. I thought he was very wise too, as if he had an old soul. Some people believe that souls come back to earth and I could imagine that he had been here before. He wore glasses, already at a young age, which is probably one of the reasons why he was bullied so much at school. He was also very smart and technical. He was able to repair electrical appliances and, when he had finished Technical School, and was fifteen years old, he already started working for an electricity shop. He was regularly hired by nearby companies when the machines didn't work. My memory is letting me down again, because I forgot the name of the electricity company he worked for. However, I do know that he also often did chores for Markus the milkman, with whom he stayed during our brief evacuation in 1944. Wim was a hard worker.

I have no idea how Wim got involved in the Resistance, but a lot of guys of his age joined, probably also students from his class and friends of his. And Wim could not stand injustice, he was very sensitive and also religious. What was happening to the Jewish people in the Netherlands, and also in Deventer itself, was something that he could not comprehend. None of us could, to be honest.

I now know that both my father, Mr. Gerritsma, and my Uncle Henk were against the Germans during the war and certainly my father carried out various actions for the Resistance, but I don't know what exactly. I also know that Wim was involved in the conversations of my father, Mr. Gerritsma and the Tensen brothers, and that he is mentioned on the two commemorative stones in Deventer and Markelo, a village near Deventer. His name is also mentioned in the appendix of the book

'De Ondergrondse' (The Resistance) by Coen Hilbrink, but there are no further details. He is then mentioned in the archives of the Dutch War Graves Foundation, but he is not mentioned in other Deventer war books. In itself this is not that surprising. As nothing was discussed in our home during the war, because it was too dangerous, and it was not discussed after the war, because it was too painful, all the information about my brother, and I suspect of many more Resistance fighters, was taken 'to the other side' so to speak – it died with them.

As far as my family is concerned, I now think that is a real shame. We cannot ask questions about it anymore. My brother Fokke was too young to remember much, my brother Laurens still has a few memories, but he too was quite young. My brother Henk, who was two years younger than me, died in 2010, so he can no longer share stories either. Wim is also mentioned on the website of 'Struikelstenen' in Deventer, an organisation that keeps the memories of war victims alive. So there is no doubt that Wim did indeed play a role in the

Resistance, all the more so when you know that the Brothers Tensen regularly came to our house, all the way from Haerst, which is thirty-eight kilometres from Deventer. This suggests that there was extensive contact between different groups of Resistance fighters. My quiet brother, who seemed a little shy and certainly wasn't aggressive, was actually playing his part in the Resistance. I keep finding it special and I am very proud of him.

My parents used to live in the city of Almelo, where Wim was born. My father and his brother Albert had a vegetable shop in Almelo, but my father left the business at one point, I don't know why. He then started repairing sewing machines and reselling them. It wasn't until the war, when we were already living in Deventer, that he started working as a collector for the Dutch Association for the Blind, perhaps because he could pass on messages for the Resistance without raising suspicion. Thinking back at it now, I can indeed imagine that this was one of the reasons he chose to become a charity collector.

In the early years of the war, my brothers Wim, Henk, Laurens and I slept in the attic. There was one bedroom at the front, with a door in the middle and a double bed, both on the right and on the left of the door. Henk and Laurens shared a bed and Wim slept in the other bed. I slept on a mattress on the floor of the attic, so not in the bedroom at the front. I slept at the rear of the attic, it was a large space that was not in use. You could even see the roof tiles. There was no heating and the winters were very cold. I remember vividly that we often would wake up in the morning and our sheets were frozen. We thought it was perfectly normal at the time.

It wasn't until after the evacuation, so sometime mid-1944, that Wim was shot in the back. It is a pity that there is not more information to be found about Wim. What exactly happened to him? How did he get home when he was hurt? Was anyone else there? Was it an ordinary German soldier, an NSB member or an SS soldier who had shot him? Was he engaged in a Resistance action or was it a stray bullet? It did sometimes happen that people were hit by stray bullets at the time. The truth, I feel, is untraceable.

I am now ninety years old and I was still a teenage boy at the time, which means that any survivors who were in the Deventer Resistance must all be way over ninety and then also have a clear memory and have known Wim. I assume the chance to find these people is nil. I also think it's normal for people of that time to bury traumatic experiences deep down inside.

To my knowledge, right after the war, there were no psychiatrists or other mental health help options for ordinary traumatised citizens and most people just wanted to forget and build a new life.

Our lives continued as normal as well after the war. However, I would like to share my scarce memories, to honour my brave brother, posthumously, so many years after the war, and preserve these stories for posterity.

After Wim was injured, he couldn't walk properly and went to sleep in the dining room where my mother had made him a bed. We, Henk,

Laurens and I, then also went downstairs to sleep in Mr. Gerritsma's bedroom. Wim was almost always in bed and my brothers and I kept him company for several hours every day. He liked that. He was very good at accepting his situation, something I thought was amazing. He got a lot of support from his faith. He also got regular visits from our then family doctor, Dr. Bruins, a big, kind man.

Today my brother Fokke and I are back in our family home. The current owners are taking us to the basement. The door is in the hallway just before the stairs turning right and then to the left. It is a special experience to be here now. The basement is very large and still exactly like it was during the war. It feels as if we are being thrown back in time.

The last months of 1944, until the liberation in May 1945, there were many bombings on Deventer and we always took shelter in the basement. The schools were already closed because it was too dangerous for pupils to go to school. When the air raid alarm went off, which happened very often, I quickly ran to the dining room where my father and I put Wim on a kitchen chair and carried him down the stairs to the cellar.

In the cellar there are two rooms with a staircase in the middle. In one of the spaces, against the wall, there is an elevated part. My father had made a bed for Wim on this. My parents, with my brother Fokke in between them, and Gré, who was still staying at our house, slept in the middle of the cellar, and Henk, Laurens and I slept side by side on the other side of the cellar, at the back of the house.

In the part where we slept was an air lattice for venting and a window. If we had to get out, in case our house had been hit by a bombing, we could have pushed the air lattice up and then crawled out the window. But luckily that was never necessary. Mr. Gerritsma continued sleeping upstairs. The secretary of the 'Ortskommandant' was already gone.

Wim's wound did not want to heal and soon after the liberation he was taken to the hospital, where they could take better care of him. There he spent the last two years of his life. My mother, my brothers Henk, Laurens and myself, went there every day to visit him. My father couldn't go every day, due to his work commitments, but he still went as many times as he could. Fokke was allowed to join once a week.

I was still a bit of a troublemaker in those years. I went to the gym and started messing around with different girlfriends. I always wanted to be the 'tough' guy. This was also the case when an old iron stove had to be carried down from the attic, which had to go to Mr. Gerritsma's office. I said to my dad "I can do it dad", but I was not able to hold onto the heavy stove when walking down and it tumbled down the stairs. With a loud bang it got stuck halfway down, through the wooden styles of the staircase. Wim laughed a lot when I told him.

He could appreciate my first motorcycle story as well. When I had just turned seventeen, I got a motorcycle from my Uncle Egbert, the brother of my father, who lived in Almelo. The motorcycle had not been used for years and was completely covered in dust. I then fixed it myself with the help of a friend who was a mechanic. After this it was still running really well despite it being an old motorcycle, a 200CC Coventry Eagle from 1930. I decided to take it to the Ford garage where I had recently started working as a typist, typing out all the invoices. I didn't have a driver's license and the motorcycle wasn't insured either. Trying to be the cool guy, I wanted to drive the motorcycle into the garage, but the garage door was closed and the brakes didn't work. The rear wheel brake rod, there were no brake cables at the time, had snapped. With my feet on the ground I tried to brake, but I shot right through the wooden and glass garage door. I was embarrassed, but I was also in shock. The motorcycle, which was severely damaged, was half inside and half outside the garage door, my hands were covered in blood. An old man, who was mopping the floor on the inside of the garage door, was so shocked that he fainted.

The mechanics in the Ford garage all laughed. Wim always enjoyed my bravura stories. I must have been exaggerating a little bit too, I'm sure.

The last months of his life Wim was only lying in bed, he could no longer get up. As his end approached, he also knew he was going to die. He was very religious and convinced that he would go to heaven. He was amazingly strong mentally and could even cheer other people up. There was a clergyman from a local Church, I remember his name, Mr. Den Ouden, who visited Wim many times. His daughter had died during the war and this man was very sad, but Wim was always very good at comforting him. He was not afraid to die at all and he died very peacefully in hospital, due to complications from his injury, on the July 25, 1947. He was twenty years old.

In the cellar Fokke and I look at the place where Wim used to sleep those last months of the war. Fokke then said: "It was summer of 1947, I was seven years old and had been staying, for a few nights, with the Brands family in the town of

Brummen. They were close friends of my parents. When I got back home, I quickly went to the pear tree in our garden and picked five beautiful, big pears. I wanted to give them to my brother Wim. I was allowed to go to the hospital once a week to visit him. I came into the kitchen with the pears and said to my mother, "I want to take these to Wim". My mother took me on her lap and said "*Wim is with our Lord Jesus*". That was all she said.".

The railway bridge

From 1942 I went to the Mulo High School in the Polstraat. This was near the quay of the river IJssel. When you walked out of school to the quay, you could see the 'pontoon bridge' on the right and about 300 metres further away, towards the village of Olst, was the railway bridge that played such an important role during the war. The first years of the war it was quite quiet and we didn't notice many activities near the bridge, but in 1944 it got serious.

Deventer was an important city for the Germans and the railway bridge in particular played a big role in this. After the Dutch defences blew up part of the railway bridge on May 10, 1940 to stop the Germans, the bridge was quickly repaired by the Occupying forces and by the end of 1940, train traffic over the bridge was possible again. This made the railway bridge a target for the Allies.

It was a bizarre time and I now realise that it was also a very dangerous time, but you cannot be afraid all the time. Everyone just continued with their daily activities, as best they could, even though the air-raid alarm went off increasingly more often. One of those air-raid alarm incidents was when we needed wood for the stove, during the winter, so that we would stay warm. My father, my Uncle Henk, my best friend Martin Groeneveld and I went to the pine forest in the Borgele district. We cut down a few large pine trees, some around twelve metres high, and we sawed them on the spot with a large saw, into two metre-long trunks. We would then cut them into smaller pieces later at home. The wood was piled onto a large handcart belonging to Mr. Gerritsma. Martin and I tied a rope around our middle and pulled the cart at the front and my father and Uncle Henk pushed the cart from behind. We were on our way home when the air-raid alarm went off. We ran home as fast as we could and went into the cellar. When it was safe to go outside we went back to pick up the cart, but someone else had already half emptied it! We had to go back to the forest the next day to cut down a few more trees.

The wailing sound of the alarm penetrated

your entire body, but in a strange way you got used to it. And we just went to school. As off 1944, especially after the summer, the frequency of the air-raid alarm increased still further. It was an almost daily happening. All the pupils at my school had to stand in the corridors of the school when the alarm went off. We were all standing with our backs against the walls. In the hallways we could hear the bomber planes of the Allies coming. I think the reason we had to stand in the hallway was because we could run away quickly if bombs were dropped too close or actually dropped on the school. This was not unthinkable, but fortunately this never happened. As we walked from school to the quay afterwards, we could see that the railway bridge was always missed, but the pontoon bridge was hit once.

From September 1944, at the same time as the Allied advance in northwest Europe, several railway and traffic bridges throughout the Netherlands were attacked by Allied bombers, including the two Deventer bridges, both the railway bridge and the pontoon bridge. However, the Germans had a strong anti-aircraft defence and we, the pupils of the Mulo High School, had contributed to that. All the boys from class three and four of our school and two teachers were ordered to come with the Germans for a few days in a row, I think this happened two or three times, to dig machine gun nests in a pasture about a hundred and fifty metres away from the railway bridge. We were divided into two groups, about ten people per group. I remember this very well. There were also other people who helped, just citizens who had been told to do so. Everybody did what they were asked, because the SS soldiers did not joke around and you simply could not say no.

We had to dig large, sloping pits in the pasture. At the front these were about a metre deep and it was half circular. We had to put reeds in that part and then braided it, so that it became a type of wicker mat. The teachers also helped with creating the pits and gave us directions. We were checked upon and guarded by two elderly German soldiers. They were actually very kind. I think these people were more than tired of the war. Of course, they were also forced to be there. I particularly remember an elderly German soldier who was always very friendly. He kept saying "Immer bitte ruhe und leise machen" (just keep calm and take it easy)... as if he wanted to say, "Don't hurry guys." One of my classmates was a big, strong boy. One day he didn't work so hard and paused for a moment. Then an SS soldier came to check on us and my classmate said "Bitte Ruhe" to him, jokingly. He was immediately beaten up really badly by the SS soldier. It was a very anxious moment. In hindsight, we could have easily overpowered the SS soldier, but if we had done something like that, reprisals would have taken place and almost certainly some parents would have been shot. Everyone knew this without having to mention it.

But I also have a great memory of one of those days digging the machine gun nests. One day, when we were all digging, a Spitfire flew over, very low. I'll never forget this. We could see the pilot and we were all waving enthusiastically and smiling at the pilot. And even one of the German soldiers willingly waved as well. The pilot saw us and waved back to us by moving the wings of the plane back and forth. He flew over the railroad bridge a few times. This was a great moment for us. This must have been towards the end of 1944 or early 1945. The Spitfire remained nearby and suddenly a steam locomotive arrived and started crossing the bridge, but the locomotive stopped right in the middle of the bridge. It must have been set up, because the train driver and the stoker got out of the train and ran away very fast. The Spitfire came back. We all stood there and watched what was happening with disbelief, but also full of excitement and with a sense of euphoria. We were about two hundred or three hundred metres away from the railway bridge. The Spitfire then shot the locomotive to shreds. He was aiming for the water tank, so the pressure went off. Such a water tank contained a lot of water which was fired with coal, and this then created the steam to power the wheels of the locomotive. When the water tank was hit, a cloud of steam escaped. We were all waving and screaming happily. The soldiers who had to check on us did not say anything, they might have been terribly scared. The Germans could no longer use the bridge for many days, because they had to tow the train away first.

Once again, I feel that it is actually a pity that I never asked my father what exactly happened during the war and what his role and the role of my brother Wim was. All that remains are the memories of my brother Laurens and myself, as my brother Fokke was too little to remember much.

Laurens remembers the munition train that stopped in front of our door. Laurens explains "I experienced the bombings on the railway bridge and other targets in the area as something I remember as being very frightening. I especially have a clear memory of when a munition train was parked in front of our house. This was in September 1944. A lot of planes from the Allied forces were flying over, trying to bomb this train. Luckily for us they missed, but a house on the other side of the train station was hit. A few days later this train was hit by bombs nearby the city of Zutphen and sadly an entire district was very badly damaged. By the end of the war, more and more planes were coming over our house. We also regularly saw the V1 bomber planes of the Germans. The V1, which stands for 'Vergeltungswaffe' (retaliatory weapon), was the first unmanned plane in the world. Thousands of V1s had been sent into the air by the Germans, targeting the Allies, but a large number of them actually landed in the Netherlands. They certainly didn't always reach their destination. So when a V1 came over, we would listen to the sound of the engine, a sign that it was still working. The sputtering sound of the plane was very recognisable. I was ten years old at the time, but it's something I've never forgotten."

From what I understand, between October 1944 and February 1945, there were a total of fourteen Allied bombing raids on Deventer. These were always carried out by several bombers at once. The strong defence of the Germans meant that the Allies had to fly very high and instead of hitting the various targets, including the railway bridge, a large part of Deventer was destroyed. Many stray bombs fell on the city and several buildings on the Diepenveenseweg, where we lived, were also hit.

Our house was never hit. Apart from the fact that the glass windows were regularly completely ruined and many roof tiles flew off our roof, due to the vibrations set off by the loud explosions of the bombings, the building remained undamaged. The first time the windows on the first and second floor, and the door broke, Uncle Henk, who was very handy, covered the windows and front door with wooden planks and made a tiny window in them, so we could still look outside. My father and I, with the help of some neighbours, had stolen these wooden planks, and also some plywood planks, from a workshop belonging to the Germans. They had seized a building about 200 metres from our house, where they had stored all types of wood. There were no Germans present at that time, because the Germans also tried to hide from the many bombs and grenades that were being thrown.

At one point it became really scary, because the building where the 'Ortskommandant' lived became a target of the Allies. He lived in a large mansion on a corner, opposite the train station and next to the 'Kweekschool' (Training College). This was very close to our house. I suspect this was in the last month of the war, when we lived in the cellar. One day a bomb fell very close to our house, I can still feel the loud bang vibrating through my body. I don't remember whether this was an attempt to flatten the mansion of the 'Ortskommandant', but it is very likely.

Now that we walk through our family home in 2019, all this seems very unreal. We walk up the stairs to the attic and my brother Fokke says he remembers standing in the cellar during an air-raid alarm. I remember that moment, too. There were also a number of German soldiers with us in the cellar. My father asked them to leave, but they didn't. Because of the huge bang, all the windows panes flew out of the window frames again and part of the roof was gone. This is one of Fokke's most intense memories. He was just a five-year-old boy at the time. He was shocked, we all were of course.

After it was safe again, we went upstairs to inspect the house for damage. When we arrived in the attic we could see the blue sky. Many roof tiles had fallen off the roof because of the impact of the bombardment. My grandfather, Grandpa Kortman, my mother's father, was with us that day and he took me with him to the roof after the bombing, to repair it as well as we could. My grandfather was standing on the roof and I was standing in the gutter, which was thirty centimetres wide and I could stand in it. This was at a height of around 10 metres. I handed the roof tiles that were still in one piece, to my grandfather and he put them in place. We covered the rest of the roof with an old piece of tarpaulin for protection so that rainwater wouldn't get into the house. We heard the grenades whizzing past us. I said to Grandpa, "What's that whizzing sound, grandpa?" And he said, "Those are grenades, my boy". We just kept working, crazy, actually!

I think my most impressive and violent memory of the entire war was the moment when the Allies made yet another attempt to destroy the railway bridge and the pontoon bridge over the river IJssel. This was on February 8, 1945. Because the bombs had to be dropped from high altitude, the targets were frequently missed. There were sixty civilian casualties in Deventer that day. A retirement home in the centre was also hit and a close friend of my parents, Mr. Ordelman, lived there. My father was asked by the Fire Brigade or the Red Cross to come to the location to help identify victims. I told my dad that I wanted to come with him, and he told me that I could. There were bodies lined up. They were covered, so that you could only see the lower part of the legs, the socks and the shoes. And when you were pretty sure who it was, you were allowed to look at the face. I remember saying to my dad, "I think this is him, Dad." People only had one pair of shoes at the time and I recognised his socks and shoes. Mr. Ordelman was indeed one of the victims. I've always pushed this memory away, but now, while

I'm telling you this, it's bothering me. I feel very emotional because I still see it in front of me. The upper body and face were covered. My father did look at the face to confirm the identification. I wasn't allowed to, and I think that's a good thing.

At the very end of the war, a very large German V2 missile, the successor to the V1, fell half a kilometre from the hospital. This was about three hundred metres from our family home. The Canadians were getting close. People were already going outside their homes a lot, expecting the Canadian military to arrive. We too often went upstairs to the bathroom to look to see whether something was happening, because from there we could see the planes going in the direction of Schalkhaar, where the Canadians had already arrived. The German occupiers tried to hit the Canadians and the Canadians fought back. The Germans still fired V1 aircrafts and V2 missiles into the air to hit England. Germany already had such missiles at the end of the war, the Allies did not. But these missiles didn't work all that perfectly and it happened regularly that instead of reaching

England, they fell straight down again. Some of these ended up in the villages of Nijverdal and Hellendoorn, as well as in other villages and towns in the region.

This large bomb fell right on top of the house of a school friend of mine, Herman Huizinga. I only knew him from gymnastics, but he sometimes came to our house. When the bomb fell, I was standing in the garage taking care of the rabbits. I was standing right beneath a wired glass roof, which is glass with steel wire. I think my guardian angel was with me, because the roof exploded into a thousand pieces, right over my head. I was standing in a sea of glass, but apart from a few tiny pieces of glass piercing my arms, I was fine. However, I was in shock. Herman Huizinga wasn't as lucky as I was. His death was particularly tragic. On the day of the Liberation, on April 10, 1945, slightly earlier than the rest of the Netherlands, there was still fighting going on between the Canadians and the Germans. Herman had gone out into the streets, just like my brothers and I and so many other people. I am sure that he too wanted to celebrate the Liberation, but he was hit by a stray bullet. He died immediately, there and then.

The Canadians

The bridges at Deventer were attacked several times by large numbers of Allied bombers. Time and time again, the bridge 'survived'. The pontoon bridge was not used much, but after German troops blew up the railway bridge themselves on April 6, 1945 just before the arrival of the Canadians in an attempt to stop the Allies, the pontoon bridge had to be reopened. Blowing up the railway bridge didn't help the Germans, as Deventer was liberated by Canadian troops on April 10, 1945. The rest of the Netherlands was liberated on May 5, 1945.

The south of the Netherlands was liberated in the autumn of 1944 by the Allies – a combination of American, Polish and Canadian armies. The liberation north of the rivers took longer, despite several attempts by the Allies. It was a very difficult winter, especially for people in the west of the Netherlands, because there was almost no food left. A lot of people ate tulip bulbs to stay alive, but many died of hunger. This was called 'De hongerwinter' (The Winter of Hunger).

February 8, 1945, marked the start of

'Operation Veritable', led by General Crerar, who had four hundred thousand British and Canadian soldiers under his command. The Canadians were mainly from the 1st Canadian infantry, which had been heading north since 1943, after landing in southern Italy, significantly overcoming German troops. Eventually, Crerar's men crossed the river Rhine heading towards Germany. The 1st Canadian infantry moved north through Germany on 7 April to enter the Netherlands via the Achterhoek, an eastern region. Passing through the towns and villages of Doesburg, Zutphen and then Gorssel, Epse, Bathmen, Colmschate and Schalkhaar, they invaded Deventer on April 10. Unfortunately, during this advance, the Canadians caused a lot of damage, because they used Crocodile tanks. These were tanks fitted with a flamethrower. They were used to set fire to farms in which German soldiers were hiding.

I remember the moment of actual Liberation very well. When we saw the first Canadian soldiers, we quickly grabbed the Dutch flag that my mother had already taken out of a cupboard, and we ran to the top floor. In the bathroom at the back of the house we put the flag out of the window. A pilot in a Spitfire, who flew over, waved at us. That was a particularly beautiful moment. From the bathroom we had a good view of what was happening. We saw several Spitfires providing air support to the Allies. The Canadians came from the same side as the Germans had arrived during their initial raid on Deventer. We were all at home when this happened, including Mr. Gerritsma. The first Canadian soldiers we saw were on foot, but they were soon followed by three tanks, equipped with Bren guns. The soldiers who were on foot had rapidly taken over and were lying on the railway embankment on our side of the railway station. The three tanks were parked in our garage, which was empty at the time.

The Canadian soldiers proceeded very carefully. They walked from porch to porch with their rifles in attack mode, in search of Germans who may have been hiding there. On the other side of the station there remained some German soldiers who were firing back. Canadian soldiers were quartered in several houses in our street and also in our house. Two soldiers with machine guns continued to stand guard in front of the windows of the dining and the living room on the first floor. Those windows still had the wooden planks with a small window in the middle. The soldiers put their machine guns through the small windows. The German soldiers on the other side of the station surrendered very quickly, that first day.

Everyone took to the streets to greet the Canadians, so did we. There was so much joy and relief, but because there was still shooting going on, this certainly was dangerous as well. In total, about ten Canadians were quartered in our house for that first night and they took turns to go to the first floor, both during the day and at night, to keep watch. I found it all very impressive and exciting. The large kitchen downstairs became a gathering point. That's where everyone came to eat and drink coffee. I remember it as if it were yesterday.

That night, my mum stayed upstairs, there was a real party atmosphere in the kitchen. There was a very big pan, that my mother always used to prepare our meals, on the table and the men poured all the spirits that they could find all thrown together, into the pan. They all had quite a few drinks. I was going to high school at the time and could already speak a little English with the Canadians. I felt very grown up, but I wasn't allowed to drink alcohol. After a few glasses of the alcoholic mixture, my dad was so drunk, he could barely walk. When the next day came, the German soldiers, who were still stationed across the train station, had either surrendered or fled, and most of the Canadian soldiers had moved on, to help liberate the rest of the Netherlands. Three shooters stayed in our house for one or two days longer, in case the Germans came back. If there still had been German soldiers in the vicinity of the station, they would have been shot, no doubt.

The first few days after the Liberation were very strange. Deventer was freed on April 10, 1945, I was fifteen years old at the time. Everyone was happy and a lot of girls from the neighbourhood had affairs with Canadian soldiers. But I also remember that men and women of the Resistance shaved the heads of so-called 'moffen girls'. These were women who had had a relationship with a German during the war. They had to walk through the city so everyone could see them. Former NSB members, who had collaborated with the Germans, were also made to walk through the streets with their hands held up. They were shouted at and insulted.

Shortly after the Liberation I found a hand grenade on the railway embankment. It was a German hand grenade and I decided to 'go fishing' with a friend in an inlet of the river IJssel, right on the other side of the train station. I threw the hand grenade into the water. I don't know how I knew, but I knew exactly what to do. A huge bang ensued and immediately about ten dead fish floated on the water. We were startled but also had to laugh uncontrollably, probably because of nerves. We didn't take the fish home as we were afraid the police would come to see what had created the loud bang. We walked home as fast as we could.

After the war, the city was slowly rebuilt. My

Uncle Henk started a shop where he repaired and sold watches. My father continued to work for the Dutch Association for the Blind, and Mr. Gerritsma continued his wholesale trade in confectionery. I had to go to school for two more years. After I had passed my exams in 1947, I went to work at Garage Haaxman, the Ford dealer in Deventer. I was seventeen years old.

My father remained a bit of a hustler, because I don't know how he managed, but when I was ordered to enlist for the army, which was compulsory service at the time, he made sure that I, and none of my brothers, had to join the army. We all got exemption because my brother Wim had died as a consequence of his work in the Resistance during the war. My brave brother Wim, I am proud of him and I hope that through these memories, which I now share with everyone, he can live on, in memory, for many years to come.

At the beginning of the war there were eleven thousand homes in Deventer, but only two and a half thousand of these houses came through the war unscathed, including our house in 'the Diepenveenseweg' No. 259 (now 18). A total of 154 civilians were killed during the bombings.

We mustn't forget

"A man is only forgotten when his name has been forgotten" is a statement on the website of 'Werkgroep Struikelstenen Deventer' (Working Group "Stumbling Stones").

During my search for information about my Uncle Wim I came across his name on the website of 'Struikelstenen Deventer.'

'Struikelstenen' can be found in both the Netherlands and other countries, such as Germany, Hungary, Austria... Originally they were called 'Stolpersteine', an initiative of German artist Gunter Demnig, also the executor of the project. He has now placed more than 35,000 stones across Europe. They are cube-shaped stones with a brass top plate engraved with a text. These stones are placed in the pavement in front of the houses in which Jews, resistance fighters and people from other minority groups lived - before or during the Second World War – and from which they had been taken and subsequently killed.

The aim of the working group in Deventer is to have these commemorative stones placed for victims of Nazi terror in Deventer. These are Jewish people, Resistance fighters, homosexuals and people who were persecuted because of their religion, such as Jehovah's Witnesses, and Roma and Sinti families. The working group also creates a personal and/or family story about the victims, which will be shared during the placement of such a commemorative stone.

After a very long search, also by 'Werkgroep Struikelstenen Deventer', it turns out that no extra information has surfaced regarding my Uncle Wim's part in or actual actions for the Resistance. There is no doubt that he was a Resistance fighter, but what exactly he did to help achieve freedom for the rest of the country remains a mystery. For this reason, sadly, it remains to be seen whether Wim will be honoured with a dedicated 'Struikelsteen' in the Diepenveenseweg.

But we will never forget him!

Epilogue by Renate

"Gosh Dad, I'd like to write a book about that," I said in May, 2019 when my father finally told me stories from when he had been a teenager, during the Second World War. These memories came to the surface after visiting the house in the Diepenveenseweg in Deventer, where they had lived during the war, together with his youngest brother Fokke.

I have chosen to tell his stories in the first person and both in the present and in the past tense. My father, a bit of a rebel - he actually still is - despite being ninety years old, has consciously experienced the war. His stories seem like adventures and in a way they were for him.

With this book, I want to show that you can't always be afraid, but that, even under extreme circumstances, life continues. However, something we see, even in today's world, is that fear is usually the basis of intolerance. If we are afraid of losing something that we consider to be ours, whether material things, or even concepts or values such as nationality, honour, faith, political identity, or culture, it is all too tempting to blame 'the other'.

Hitler was a master of manipulation and sadly, in my opinion, we see these types of figures arising once again in current politics around the world. Ostensibly intelligent, they slowly but surely rouse that feeling of 'we are better than them, we have more rights than them'. If you mention that often enough, there will be many people who are going to believe it. Intolerance is a symptom of fear and this quickly translates into an insensitivity towards the 'other'. They are 'dehumanised'. And people who consider themselves generous, honest and humane, can suddenly come to hate fellow citizens of different nationality or faith, even small children, and become immune to what happens to these people.

What happened in Europe in 1940 to 1945 still takes place in many parts of this world. Fortunately, there is also a lot of good happening, and there are those who want to fight this injustice, and stand up against this intolerance, like my father's family during the war. We must never defend injustice or an act of terror, whether this concerns a raid on a country, killing an entire ethnic group, suicide bombings or individual acts of terror in the name of a religion. These are things that we should definitely fight against and, if possible, nip in the bud. But generalising doesn't work.

Not all Germans were bad or dangerous, the secretary of the 'Ortskommandant' was in bed with a young man from the Resistance... The German soldier who was shot dead in the Second World War, seventeen years young, for refusing to kill Resistance men and women of his own age, was not a bad man. Not all Muslims are bad or dangerous. Not all immigrants are bad or dangerous. Most seek a better life in another country, away from danger in their homeland or poor economic conditions. Most want to work, build a new life and contribute to the economy.

I am an immigrant, too. I have lived in Israel, New Zealand and Italy and now I have lived in Spain for over 18 years. Here, too, I have witnessed some subtle intolerance towards foreigners. I am one of them. I know what it feels like not to be fully accepted. It is part of the status of immigrant and yes, even as a Dutch person in Spain in a small village you never quite belong. Not even if you're married to a kind Spanish man, as I am. But one thing I know for sure, this too, is based on fear and prejudice. The only way to break that pattern is to get to know each other with respect, with curiosity, and eventually with open arms. Most people are good, I still believe that. Ask yourself, which group would you rather be a part of?

Renate

Source information

http://www.nederlandstegelmuseum.nl

https://mooifriesland.nl

https://oorlogsgravenstichting.nl

https://shoppenindeventer.nl/2017/05/03/deventer-in-oorlogstijd/

http://www.struikelstenen-deventer.nl

http://struikelstenen.nl/

https://nl.wikipedia.org/wiki/Geschiedenis_van_Deventer

https://nl.wikipedia.org/wiki/Schipbrug_Deventer

http://www.plankenloodsje.nl

http://www.genne.nl

https://www.verzetsmuseum.org

https://www.facebook.com/HerinnerJeDeventer

https://www.battlefieldtours.nu/informatie/operation-cannonshot/

A special thanks to Suzanne Elizabeth Saunter Clark and Susie James.